This book belongs to Eric Owens

the art of the daydream

the art of the daydream

WENDY BRISTOW

MQP

Published by **MQ Publications Limited**
12 The Ivories
6–8 Northampton Street
London N1 2HY
Tel: 44 (0) 20 7359 2244
Fax: 44 (0) 20 7359 1616
email: mail@mqpublications.com
website: www.mqpublications.com

Design by **Balley Design Associates**

ISBN: 1 84072 621 0   Printed and bound in China

1 3 5 7 9 0 8 6 4 2

*This book contains the opinions and ideas of the author.
It is intended to provide helpful and informative
material on the subjects addressed in this book and is
sold with the understanding that the author and
publisher are not engaged in rendering medical, health,
or any other kind of personal professional services in this
book. The reader should consult his or her medical, health,
or competent professional before adopting any of the
suggestions in this book or drawing references from it.
The author and publisher disclaim all responsibility for
any liability, loss, or risk, personal or otherwise, which is
incurred as a consequence, directly or indirectly, of the use
and application of any of the contents of this book.*

Contents

Introduction **6**

1 Why do we need to daydream? **8**

2 Why some people daydream more than others **36**

3 How to make the most of it **54**

Introduction

DREAMS ARE TRUE WHILE THEY LAST, AND DO WE NOT LIVE IN DREAMS?

Alfred Lord Tennyson

"Stop staring out of the window!" "Are you listening?" "Pay attention at the back!" Often the messages we get about daydreaming in our society are negative ones.

The pressures on our snatched daydreaming moments are negative, too, reflecting the fact that we live in a world where contemplation, switching off, having a little head space to ourselves, spending a moment with our own private thoughts and fantasies is undervalued. Increasingly, we're distracted. By cell phones—so we're gossiping (or texting) when we used to be gazing. By computer games —so our brain is on when it used to be off. By all those channels on cable TV—so tempting when we have a spare minute. In Singapore, there are even little TVs in the cabs and buses—so people can never get away from stimulation. For centuries, getting from A to B has been a time when your mind could make journeys of its own. But now it's very hard to escape input.

Doing, as well as distraction, is the enemy of daydreaming. Whether child or adult, male or female, we are all too busy rushing around, multitasking, achieving. It's contagious. Our lives are too tightly jammed and scheduled with projects, goals, ideas, meetings, appointments and commitments, expectations and obligations, duties, chores, ought-tos, have-tos, and must-sees.

Life is speeding up and we're always on the go. I've noticed how friends ask one another "Are you busy?" these days as though not to be would be a terrible thing. I even get e-mails in which "Hope you're busy" is a sign-off like "Have a nice day." Children are ferried from one organized activity to another. There's less playing on the street, more organized sports.

As a result, people are speedier and speedier. A recent psychological experiment asked people to be still and tell the researcher when they thought a minute had passed. The worst result was 16 seconds!

Yet there's a whole body of evidence that says doing nothing, daydreaming, staring off into the middle distance, is one of the things that keep us sane. That done in moderation and not as an escape from reality, it's profoundly good for us. What are we missing out on if we don't do it? That's what this book is about—what we're missing out on and how to get it back.

Our truest life is when we are in dreams awake.

Henry David Thoreau

1

ALMOST ALL NEW IDEAS HAVE AN ASPECT OF FOOLISHNESS WHEN THEY ARE FIRST PRODUCED.

Alfred North Whitehead

Why do we need to daydream?

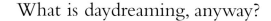

What is daydreaming, anyway?

Yale psychology professor Jerome L. Singer formulates a good definition in his book *Daydreaming and Fantasy*:

Daydreaming represents a shift of attention away from some primary physical or mental task we have set for ourselves, or away from directly looking at or listening to something in the external environment, toward an unfolding sequence of private responses made to some internal stimulus. The inner processes usually considered are "pictures in the mind's eye," the unrolling of a sequence of events, memories or creatively constructed images of future events which have varying degrees of probability of taking place.

THE SUBCONSCIOUS IS CEASELESSLY MURMURING, AND IT IS BY LISTENING TO THESE MURMURS THAT ONE HEARS THE TRUTH.

Gaston Bachelard

What happens when we daydream?

Daydreaming is a state when the brain is between alpha and beta waves but not yet asleep. So the mind is less focused and roams from one topic to another or mulls over one topic without a specific agenda. It is a way of allowing yourself to play with ideas without focusing on real scenarios, motivations, or outcomes—a sort of "what if?" state of mind. It produces the right frame of mind to unconsciously incubate previously received and stored information and to stumble across solutions and ideas that we often call intuition.

What goes on in the brain when we daydream? There are four categories of brain waves, ranging from those displaying the most activity to those with the least activity. When the brain is aroused and actively engaged in mental activities, it generates beta waves, the fastest of the four different brain waves. Beta waves are characteristics of a strongly engaged mind. A person talking would be in beta. A debater would be in high beta.

Next in order of frequency is alpha. Where beta represented arousal, alpha represents nonarousal. Alpha brain waves are slower. Someone who has finished a task and sits down to take a break is often in an alpha state. Someone who takes time out to reflect or meditate is usually in alpha.

Then come theta brain waves, which are even slower. Someone who is daydreaming is often in a theta brain wave state. Drivers who discover they can't recall the last five miles are often in a theta state, induced by the brain-numbing process of motorway driving.

Repetitive action—whether motorway driving, running, walking, or even taking a shower where the water pulses on your skin—can put you in a theta state, which is why good ideas often pop up during these activities. It is a state in which tasks become so automatic that you can mentally disengage from them. Theta thoughts are usually free-flowing and occur without censorship or guilt—they represent a positive mental state, where anything is possible. The final brain wave state is delta— and that's when you're fast asleep.

A secret solace

One of the interesting things about daydreaming is that it takes a quantum leap from one kind of thinking or consciousness to another—a quantum leap because there is no process in between. Often we don't know we're doing it, or we don't notice we've drifted off, until that vacant look in our eyes makes it easily recognizable to others and we suddenly realize we're doing it from our teacher's raised voice, our boss's sarcasm, or our partner's ranting.

The mind is not like a computer, it is neither on or off. And if the stimulation it's getting is not engaging its interest, it will think of something else. One researcher found we daydream for between 10 and 20 percent of our waking hours, depending on the nature of the task—the longer we do the same thing, the more likely we are to daydream. Several researchers (Giambra; Smallwood; Klinger and Cox) have noted its relationship to boredom: the lower the demand of the task, the more likely we are to daydream.

And why not?

The wonderful—and unique—thing about daydreaming is that it's invisible. We can't enter another's daydreams and see what they are like. Sometimes other people do know we're "away with the fairies," but we can also keep to ourselves the fact that we're off somewhere else. Hence our daydreams are the most private part of us. We have them in solitude. No one can know our daydreams, unless we tell them. And daydreams are where we meet ourselves.

Geniuses do it

Genius physicist Albert Einstein was, in his own words, "disorderly and a dreamer." The inventor of the theory of relativity thought he had his best ideas in the shower and so installed waterproof writing materials so he could jot them down at once. Einstein's most famous theory came to him during a "thought experiment," by his imagining what it would be like to ride on a beam of light.

When asked why it was he who dreamed up the theory of relativity, Einstein said: "The reason, I think, is that a normal adult never stops to think about problems of space and time. These are things which he has thought of as a child. But my intellectual development was retarded, as a result of which I began to wonder about space and time only when I had already grown up. Naturally, I could go deeper into the problem than a child with normal abilities."

Einstein's ability to hold onto the child's wonder about the world, and childish "thought experiments" led to massive breakthroughs in the areas of quantum physics and atomic energy.

Einstein's whole approach to science was embedded in what we do when we daydream. He said: "…one of the strongest motives that lead a person to art and science is flight from everyday life, with its painful harshness and wretched dreariness."

I want to know God's thoughts… the rest are details.

Albert Einstein

DON'T LET ANYBODY TELL YOU YOU'RE WASTING YOUR TIME WHEN YOU'RE GAZING INTO SPACE. THERE IS NO OTHER WAY TO CONCEIVE AN IMAGINARY WORLD. I NEVER SIT DOWN IN FRONT OF A BARE PAGE TO INVENT SOMETHING. I DAYDREAM ABOUT MY CHARACTERS, THEIR LIVES AND THEIR STRUGGLES, AND WHEN A SCENE HAS BEEN PLAYED OUT IN MY IMAGINATION AND I THINK I KNOW WHAT MY CHARACTERS FELT, SAID AND DID, I TAKE PEN AND PAPER AND TRY TO REPORT WHAT I'VE WITNESSED.

Stephen Vizinczey

All great works of art were daydreams first and foremost

In the imaginative realm of fantasy, nothing is impossible. And it's allowing this quality of possibility, mulling it over in your mind, that facilitates the kind of thoughts no one has ever thought before you sat there and thought them.

Writing a novel doesn't begin with the first word written down. The stupendously successful *Harry Potter* series began with author J. K. Rowling staring out of the window on a long train ride between London and Edinburgh. She happened to have a notebook handy when her daydreams turned to thoughts and, by the end of the journey, she had the plot for the first novel. But she did not sit on that train and *plan* to think up a novel. It began with her emptying her brain. If J. K. Rowling had had a cellphone, a novel, or a laptop with her to distract her, Harry Potter might never have been born—and children the world over would have missed out on a lot of magic.

This is how artists do the rest of us a service by daydreaming on behalf of all of us. Artists collate the daydreams of the collective, and, in turn, fuel our daydreams by giving us more characters to daydream about. Now we're Luke Skywalker, fighting with the force. Now we're Elizabeth Bennet, picking over our feelings for Mr. Darcy. Now we're Billy Liar, making our daydreams real—and, yes, getting in a right mess!

It's the first stage of making anything happen

As with all great works of art, so with the work of art that is your life. You have to daydream about moving house before you can actually do it. You will need to visualize the end result and imagine running that marathon to actually get yourself through all the training and keep staggering through to the end. Insistent daydreams that interfere with your boring job and see you in another career you'd love to try are what's needed to give you the impetus to actually retrain.

Sports coaches use the power of daydreaming to enable athletes to get to that winning post. They encourage their charges to imagine every step of the winning process in great detail, utilizing all the senses, even feeling the effort in all of their muscles.

Psychologists say that daydreams improve our ability to delay immediate pleasures so future goals can be achieved. If you can imagine the future gain that will result from, say, not eating that cream cake right now—if you can imagine yourself slimmer in the future—you can leave that cake on the plate.

Also, any kind of change engages daydreaming. What will it be like when I'm doing that new job? Living in that new house? Nursing my father through this illness? You think it, then you live it.

IF YOU DON'T HAVE A DREAM, IF YOU DON'T HAVE A DREAM? HOW YOU GONNA HAVE A DREAM COME TRUE?

Rodgers and Hammerstein

It balances the brain

We live in a left-brain-dominated society. The brain is divided into two halves, connected by a thick cable of nerves at the base of the brain called the *corpus collosum*. There is a school of thought that believes the left side of the brain is the part responsible for logical, rational thought, and verbal input; the right side for nonverbal, spatial thought, flashes of insight, and creativity. Maths versus drawing. Planning versus mulling.

Left Brain	Right Brain
Logical	Random
Sequential	Intuitive
Rational	Holistic
Analytical	Synthesizing
Objective	Subjective
Looks at parts	Looks at wholes
Likes words	Likes pictures
Order/pattern perception	Spatial perception
Thinking things through	Flashes of insight
Works with information	Works with feelings

Science today favors logical, empirical evidence that we can think through and prove. Our state education system still emphasizes reading, writing, and arithmetic, the three left-brain functions, and places less emphasis on artistic, esthetic, spatial, and symbolic thought and information. Analysis and accuracy—left-brain functions—are valued over feeling, "sensing," and intuition—right-brain functions.

The minute you visualize something in your head, you're using the right side of the brain. You're giving the logical half a rest, allowing for creative thoughts to come in, even when you're not actively "thinking" them through. Indulging in right-brain activity like daydreaming gives the overworked left brain a break and prevents us from turning into logic-dominated robots.

Little Dulce, tired of play, lay fast asleep in the nest she had made in one of the haycocks close by, and Rose leaned against the gnarled old tree, dreaming daydreams with her work at her feet. Happy and absorbing fancies they seemed to be, for her face was beautifully tranquil, and she took no heed of the train which suddenly went speeding down the valley, leaving a white cloud behind.

Louisa May Alcott

It makes us feel better

Clinical psychologist Jerome Singer carried out a study of daydreaming that found that most people daydream sometime during the day and identified the two most common daydream scenarios. These were the "conquering hero" and the "suffering martyr" themes.

In the conquering hero fantasy, the daydreamer lands the starring role as the rich, famous movie star, Superman, Mr. Perfect, the guy who gets the girl, the contract, and the Ferrari. Themes like these, said Singer, seem to reflect the need for mastery and escape from the frustrations of everyday life.

Suffering another other type of daydream known as martyr daydreams, on the other hand, offer wallowing-in-misery-style scenarios that center on feelings of being neglected, hurt, rejected, or unappreciated by others. In these fantasies the people who did us wrong end up regretting their past actions and realizing what wonderful people we are after all. The extreme of this kind of scenario is the "they'll miss me when I'm gone" story. Now don't tell me you've never had that one once or twice!

This same Yale professor, Jerome Singer, found that, in most people, fantasy and daydreaming are associated with positive emotional adjustment, lower levels of aggression, and greater mental flexibility or creativity.

It makes wishes come true—at least in your head

The father of psychology, Sigmund Freud, believed daydreaming was about wish-fulfillment and a form of adult play. While children play openly and with real things (dolls, toys, computer games), adults play more covertly via fantasizing because it's no longer acceptable for them to play "dress up dolly." Another factor is that much of adult play and wish-fulfillment is about wishes that we wouldn't want others to know about. Freud implied that adults have lost a healthy relationship with their own desires (and playfulness).

To Freud, a novel or a work of art was little more than wish-fulfillment on the part of the writer or artist. However,

as daydreaming guru Jerome Singer points out, Freud and his contemporaries' conclusions were drawn from observing their patients, who were always people with emotional problems, and not via what we would today call empirical proven scientific experiment.

Freud also said daydreaming is a form of "trial action." It's true that we do rehearse conversations with significant others, experiment with and check out the likelihood of telling our boss we're leaving for a brilliant new job, and imagine what we'd do if we won the lottery or Prince William proposed marriage. Well, some of us do.

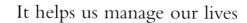

It helps us manage our lives

We know now that daydreaming is one of the main ways that we organize our lives, learn from our experiences, and plan for our futures....Daydreams really are a window on the things we fear and the things we long for in life.

Eric Klinger, psychologist and author of the book *Daydreaming*

Daydreaming is a way of doing your mental filing or processing during the day. There's a theory that says you sleep better if you've done mental filing regularly during the day—because then you don't have to do it at night. Some insomniacs can't sleep because they haven't done this "filing."

Daydreaming is quite necessary. Without it, the mind couldn't get done all the thinking it has to do during a normal day....You can't possibly do all your thinking with a consciousness (that is constantly distracted). Instead, your unconscious mind is working out problems all the time.

Leonard Giambra, psychologist

Daydreaming, then, may be one way that the unconscious and conscious minds have silent dialogues.

It creates business success

Henry Ford, the father of twentieth-century American industry and the inventor of mass production, was a firm supporter of daydreaming. The motor car magnate once called in an efficiency expert, who recommended firing an employee who was always daydreaming with his feet on his desk whenever the expert passed his office. Ford told him that the employee's last idea had dramatically increased sales. "Let him daydream," he said.

More recently, America's General Electric company, often ahead of everyone else in business practices, introduced a "Take Five" program in which all employees would spend five minutes a day thinking about the company's future. Then they would share the ideas they'd had. According to Hamel's "law of innovation" it takes a thousand ideas to generate a hundred experiments that create ten funded projects that result in one business success. That's a lot of daydreaming!

Reverie is when ideas float in our mind without reflection or regard of the understanding.

John Locke

All things in moderation

Like many things we enjoy, daydreaming isn't always good for us. It's best enjoyed in moderation and used positively.

Used negatively, it can be an escape from everyday life, a refuge into fantasy as a way of not dealing with reality. There is a time and a place for everything, and if we're daydreaming when we should be finishing that report, and daydreaming wins out, the results will not be good. Moreover, persistent daydreaming is a symptom of some psychiatric conditions, as is conjuring up a fantasy and believing that it is reality.

Daydreaming that replaces action, by promising that the dream will be reality, is obviously not to be recommended. Just like dreaming about winning the lottery rather than facing up to that massive pile of bills that haven't been paid.

Part of the "art" of daydreaming is to know when enough is enough. Some of us don't daydream enough, while some of us are daydreaming junkies who prefer our inner, imaginary world to the real one.

Then there are those of us whose daydreams tend to the apocalyptic. So when our boss offers a mild criticism, we see ourselves losing our job, becoming homeless, and living on the street. Our partner gives us a funny look and it's divorce, which of course means we'll end up homeless and living on the street. All of this gives us a slight headache and, of course, to us that's a brain tumor….

Psychotherapists call these "catastrophic fantasies." Imagining the worst and obsessing over the negative aspect of anything, is not good daydreaming, especially as there's a whole school of thought that says we bring about what we focus our thoughts upon.

Jerome Singer found that people who scored highly on what he called "guilty, negatively-toned emotional daydreams" were also those whose thoughts and fantasies "take on a strongly ethical tone, full of self-doubt and self-questioning." Interestingly, many of these people were still highly successful, being driven by a fear of failure more than a belief in success. But one thing is sure: your stress levels will be higher if you're always imagining the world is about to collapse around you.

CREATIVE POWERS CAN JUST AS EASILY TURN OUT TO BE DESTRUCTIVE. IT RESTS SOLELY WITH THE MORAL PERSONALITY WHETHER THEY APPLY THEMSELVES TO GOOD THINGS OR TO BAD. AND IF THIS IS LACKING, NO TEACHER CAN SUPPLY IT OR TAKE ITS PLACE.

Carl Jung

That minister of ministers,
Imagination, gathers up
The undiscovered Universe,
Like jewels in a jasper cup.

Imagination, new and strange
In every age, can turn the year;
Can shift the poles and lightly change
The mood of men, the world's career.

John Davidson

Jung and the collective unconscious

Swiss psychologist Carl Jung was a student of Freud and a great dreamer himself. Like Freud, Jung psychoanalyzed himself over his long life, and not only was he fascinated by his dreams, daydreams, and visions, but they also fueled his groundbreaking theories about the nature of consciousness.

Jung had a capacity for very lucid dreams and occasional visions. In the fall of 1913, he had a vision of a "monstrous flood" engulfing most of Europe and lapping at the mountains of his native Switzerland. He saw thousands of people drowning and civilization crumbling. Then the waters turned into blood. This was followed by similar nightmares. Unsurprisingly, Jung feared for his own mental health.

But the next year World War I broke out and Jung believed there had been a connection, somehow, between his individual self and humanity at large that couldn't be explained away. The experience led him to formulate his theory of the collective unconscious. Freud had "discovered" the unconscious—a part of us that we're mostly unaware of but that contains our instincts and all the things we'd rather not look at, which may surface in our dreams. Jung took it one step further and argued that humanity itself has a collective unconscious that we may all tap into, stuffed with the memories, experiences, and drives of humankind. His visions accessed this collective unconscious, which, it seemed, was preparing for and worrying about war.

Jung recorded his dreams, fantasies, and visions, and his most famous book is an autobiography called *Memories, Dreams, and Reflections*. He also painted and sculpted them. He found his dreamworld experiences featured certain central characters, such as a wise old man and a little girl, a dwarf guarding the entrance to the unconscious, and a hero figure. From this Jung concluded that the unconscious is peopled by archetypal figures—respectively, the guide, the feminine soul or "anima," "the shadow," and the "hero" or "animus."

Jung's theories have been hugely influential on everything from storytelling to advertising. When we recognize certain symbols (the cross, the star of David) or intuit the meanings of certain myths (the hero's going to get the girl), we're tapping into the collective unconscious. When we cheer on Luke Skywalker and hiss at Darth Vadar, Jung would say we're responding to archetypes (hero, shadow) in the collective unconscious. He'd be proud to know his theories influenced the storytelling guru Joseph Campbell who, in turn, counseled *Star Wars* director George Lucas, so that Luke et al. are *purposely* reflecting Jung's archetypes. The phenomenal worldwide success of the *Star Wars* series shows Jung's theories do work—we all love an archetype and they do people our own dreams.

So she sat on, with closed eyes, and half believed herself in Wonderland, though she knew she had but to open them again, and all would change to dull reality—the grass would be only rustling in the wind, and the pool rippling to the waving of the reeds—the rattling teacups would change to tinkling sheep-bells, and the Queen's shrill cries to the voice of the shepherd boy—and the sneeze of the baby, the shriek of the Gryphon, and all the other queer noises, would change (she knew) to the confused clamor of the busy farm-yard—while the lowing of the cattle in the distance would take the place of the Mock Turtle's heavy sobs.

Lastly, she pictured to herself how this same little sister of hers would, in the after-time, be herself a grown woman; and how she would keep, through all her riper years, the simple and loving heart of her childhood; and how she would gather about her other little children, and make their eyes bright and eager with many a strange tale, perhaps even with the dream of Wonderland of long ago; and how she would feel with all their simple sorrows, and find a pleasure in all their simple joys, remembering her own child-life, and the happy summer days.

Lewis Carroll

2

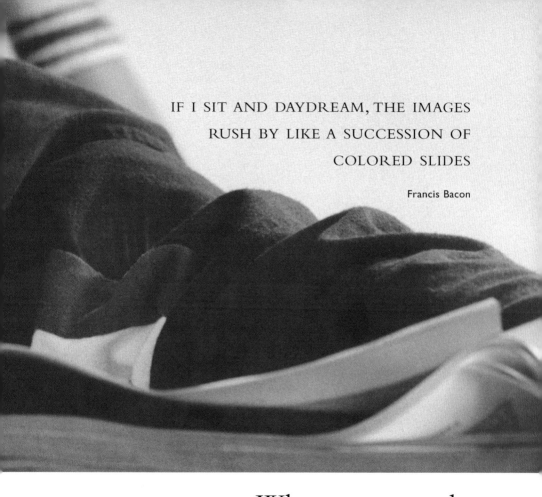

IF I SIT AND DAYDREAM, THE IMAGES
RUSH BY LIKE A SUCCESSION OF
COLORED SLIDES

Francis Bacon

Why some people
daydream more than others

Jung's four types

Another of Jung's theories posited that there are four basic personality types.

It begins with the distinction between introversion and extroversion. Introverts prefer their internal world of thoughts, feelings, fantasies, dreams, and so on, while extroverts prefer the external world of things and people and activities. Already we can see that introverts are more likely to daydream than extroverts, who are so busy out in the world that they rarely get the time.

Then Jung believed there are four ways of seeing and receiving the world that either an introvert or extrovert might favor and orient towards.

Sensing: getting information via the senses. A sensing person is good at looking and listening and generally getting to know the world. This often involves perceiving, rather than judging, information. Sensing types have very sensitive powers of observation.

Thinking: evaluating information or ideas rationally and logically. This involves rational decision making or judging, rather than simple intake of information.

Intuiting: a kind of perception that works outside of the usual conscious processes. It is perceptual, like sensing, but comes from the complex integration of large amounts of information, rather than from simple seeing or hearing. Jung said it was like seeing around corners. The intuitive type doesn't think things through but acts on "gut feeling," "intuitive flashes," and "hunches."

Feeling: like thinking, a way of evaluating information, this time by weighing up one's overall, emotional response to life.

We all have these functions, but we have them to different degrees. Each of us has what Jung called a superior function, which we favor and practice most. Then a secondary function, which we're aware of and use to support our superior function; a tertiary function, slightly less developed but not very conscious; and lastly an inferior function, which we're not very good at and which is unconscious.

So someone with intuiting as their superior function is likely to spend a lot more time daydreaming than a thinking type who is busy doing beta-type puzzling, or a sensing type who is observing the world around them, or a feeling type who is checking in with their emotions. Ideas coming to us "in a flash," as they do when we are daydreaming, is a characteristic of the intuiting type.

While most of us develop only one or two of these functions, Jung believed our goal should be to develop all four.

SERYOZHA LOOKED INTENTLY AT THE TEACHER, AT HIS SCANTY BEARD, AT HIS SPECTACLES, WHICH HAD SLIPPED DOWN BELOW THE RIDGE ON HIS NOSE, AND FELL INTO SO DEEP A REVERIE THAT HE HEARD NOTHING OF WHAT THE TEACHER WAS EXPLAINING TO HIM.

Leo Tolstoy

Creative geniuses

Film director Ang Lee, best known for *Crouching Tiger, Hidden Dragon, The Ice Storm*, and *Sense and Sensibility*, who once likened himself to "watercress floating on the water," was an absent-minded student. He often left his schoolbag on the bus and had trouble focusing on daily life. "I was so spaced out," he says of lunch at school one day, "I fell back in my chair, literally tipped over."

The great poet T. S. Eliot was once asked why he didn't go to see movies more often. "Because," he said, "they interfere with my daydreams."

A series of studies in New York City schools and colleges found that creative adolescents who excelled at art or writing showed greater openness to imagination and were more likely to have had imaginary friends in their early childhood than equally talented young people without creative achievements.

Creative geniuses often have their breakthrough insights by pondering two disparate things and making an association. And this is more likely to come about by "mulling" on things rather than actively thinking them through. If Albert Einstein had stuck to the math, and not made that imaginary journey on a beam of light, he might never have come up with the theory of relativity.

Genius, in truth, means little more than the faculty of perceiving in an unhabitual way.

William James

People with boring jobs

As mentioned in the introduction, if you do a job that emphasizes routine, monotonous tasks, you're more likely to daydream. Unsurprisingly, one of the benefits of daydreaming is that it fills a need for stimulation when you're doing the same thing over and over. You might be checking bottles in a production line, but in your head you're Marilyn Monroe singing "Happy Birthday" to JFK. As Marilyn herself said (quoting Oscar Wilde): "We are all in the gutter, but some of us are looking at the stars."

For people carrying out routine tasks, daydreaming not only provides stimulation, but may even keep them awake. One experiment done by Jerome Singer asked people to perform very dull tasks for an hour and a half. Half the group were told to count repeatedly from one to nine, while the other half were encouraged to speak their daydreams out loud. The two groups performed equally well, but the former kept getting drowsy and dropping off, while the second remained alert and perky.

This suggests that when we're bored, daydreaming may provide a trade-off. At the cost of taking up some of your attention and making you slightly less aware of what is going on around you, it keeps you more aroused and ready for action. For example, a daydreaming lifeguard might be slower getting to swimmers in trouble, but at least he hasn't dropped off and missed them.

DREAM LOFTY DREAMS, AND AS YOU DREAM, SO YOU SHALL
BECOME. YOUR VISION IS THE PROMISE OF WHAT YOU SHALL ONE
DAY BE; YOUR PROPHECY OF WHAT YOU SHALL AT LAST UNVEIL.

James Lane Allen

Cultural climate

Daydreaming can be a cultural thing. Cultural values that hold reason, logic, and numbers as good; playfulness for children only; fantasy as a waste of time; intuition, daydreaming, pleasure, and humor as bad, all act as a common barrier to creative thinking.

The culture keenest on daydreaming is probably that of the Australian Aborigines. The Aboriginals way of life is determined by the concept of "Dreamtime," which encompasses past, present, and future and is always in the spirit of creation. Places were named according to the type of dreaming you could do there. The ocean, for example, would be a place of sea-dreaming.

Nineteenth- and twentieth-century Western culture (and probably twenty-first), with its emphasis on facts, science, and technology has not been greatly in favor of daydreaming. Early psychologists ignored it as a subject of study for years, regarding it, if they regarded it at all, as a symptom of mental illness. It is only since the 1970s that psychologists have begun to study the subject and discovered the benefits that accrue from seemingly doing nothing other than staring into space.

SHE CAME OUT OF HER REVERIE WITH A DEEP SIGH AND LOOKED AT HIM WITH THE DREAMY GAZE OF A SOUL THAT HAD BEEN WONDERING AFAR, STAR–LED.

L. M. Montgomery

New lovers

When we fall in love, even the most rational computer-brain types are liable to spend moments rapt in reverie, oblivious to the reality of the salesgirl asking for their money in the coffee shop and totally immersed in the wonder of their beloved's coconut-scented hair. Some get so carried away with their ideal daytime fantasies that they find themselves married with 2.4 children before they've even had a second date.

Why do new lovers daydream so much, seeing wonderful possibilities in their new partner? It seems to be a crucial stage of falling in love, but why do it?

Psychologists believe that it's nature's way of conning us into mating with someone we might not like so much—and hence make a biological commitment to—if we could see them in the cold light of day, hairy warts and all.

When we are love-struck, a chemical—PEA (phenylethylamine)—is released in our brains that provides a burst of elation and enables us to view our beloved through rose-tinted glasses. The very longest our brains can produce PEA continuously in a relationship is two years. After it wears off, we are much less likely to daydream about the possibilities of this affair and more likely to settle into a calmer love, grounded in a more realistic appraisal and acceptance of our partner's virtues and faults.

I've met a wonderful man. He's fictional, but you can't have everything.

Mia Farrow's character in Woody Allen's film *The Purple Rose of Cairo*

People who are close to their mothers

Two major daydreaming studies have found that women and men who are mummy's girls and boys tend to daydream more often than children closer to their fathers. Why should this be? Jerome Singer says: "To some extent mothers in our society tend to represent inhibition of impulses and also to foster aesthetic or spiritual interests, while fathers are more likely to represent action tendencies within the family structure and also to be the agents of the external environment. Closer identification with the mother figure would therefore appear particularly likely to be related to fantasy or daydreaming tendencies."

Singer carried out two studies in this area, one on women and one on both sexes. These studies found that those people who reported themselves as more similar to, and/or closer to, their mothers than their fathers daydreamed more frequently. Those people who said they were more similar to, and/or closer to, their fathers were more concerned with doing than dreaming.

Thomas Edison's method

How many geniuses does it take to invent a lightbulb? One: Thomas Edison, the prolific American inventor who notched up a total of 1,093 patents during his lifetime, including ones for silent movies, talking pictures, the lightbulb, and, most significantly since in 1884 it changed the world, the first practical centralized power system for generating heat, light, and power.

His method? Edison would consciously attempt to put his brain into a state where theta brain waves would work for him. He would doze off in a chair with his arms and hands draped over the armrests. In each hand he held a ball bearing. Below each hand on the floor were two pie plates. When he drifted into the state between waking and sleeping, his hands would naturally relax and the ball bearings would drop onto the plates. Awakened by the noise, Edison would immediately make notes on any ideas that had come to him.

Edison, by the way, was almost totally deaf from his youth onward. But when offered the chance to have his hearing restored, the great inventor refused. His rationale behind this was that he was afraid he "would have difficulty relearning how to channel his thinking in an ever more noisy world."

The Possible's slow fuse is lit
By the Imagination.

Emily Dickinson

Isolated children

Children who are relatively isolated often end up daydreaming more. Singer found that children without siblings do it more frequently than those with siblings. Not only do they have more opportunity because of the time they spend alone, but they also need to develop more ways of entertaining themselves.

In his memoir *This Boy's Life* (made into a film starring Robert De Niro and Leonardo DiCaprio), only-child author Tobias Wolff poignantly describes his solitary daydreams as a young boy. "Most afternoons I wandered around in the trance habitual solitude induces. I walked downtown and stared at the merchandise. I imagined being adopted by different people I saw on the street. Sometimes, seeing a man in a suit come toward me from a distance that blurred his features, I would prepare myself to recognize my father and be recognized by him. Then we would pass each other and a few minutes later I would pick someone else."

Teenagers

Unsurprisingly, daydreaming activity peaks in late adolescence and declines with age. The elderly do still daydream, but the content of their reveries is far more likely to be reminiscence than, say, hero stories or winning the lottery. Once we hit adulthood, daydreaming falls off sharply in most people, partly because of all the rushing around involved in raising children and maintaining a home and career; partly because, as Singer puts it, "Even in its more fantastic aspects daydreaming involves some orientation toward the probable." The more settled our lives become, the more we know how are lives are going to be, the less likely we are to dream of making them different. We accept, not yearn.

Of course, one of the other obvious reasons why teenagers might daydream so often is that they also tend to fall in love so often (see page 45).

...HER MOST SERIOUS SHORTCOMING SEEMED TO BE A
TENDENCY TO FALL INTO DAYDREAMS IN THE MIDDLE OF
A TASK AND FORGET ALL ABOUT IT UNTIL SUCH TIME AS
SHE WAS SHARPLY RECALLED TO EARTH BY A REPRIMAND
OR A CATASTROPHE.

L. M. Montgomery

How daydreaming helped save a life
(and founded a whole movement)

Victor Frankl was a psychologist raised in Freud's tradition, which held that whatever happens to you as a child shapes your whole life. Frankl was a Jew living in Vienna at the time of the Nazi invasion and he was sent to the concentration camps, including Auschwitz.

His parents, his brother, and his wife all died in the camps or the gas ovens. Frankl himself barely escaped death, never knowing if he was to be one of the "saved" who removed the bodies, or one of the bodies himself.

One day, naked and alone in a small room, he realized that he possessed what he called "the last of the human freedoms"—the one his persecutors couldn't take from him. This was his freedom to choose his reaction to what was happening, and his ability to observe himself as all this was going on.

When things got really bad, Frankl used this last freedom to daydream himself out of it. He would imagine himself lecturing to his students after his release from the camps, picturing himself in the classroom giving lessons he was learning during his very torture. Moreover, he noticed that, among those of his fellow prisoners given a chance for survival, it was those who held onto a vision of the future—whether a significant task before them, or a return to their loved ones—who were most likely to survive their suffering.

Later, when Frankl was released and he did lecture again to students, he formulated a theory that it is not just what happens to us, but the meaning we take from those experiences that shapes who we are. He founded existential psychology and logotherapy, based on his concentration camp experiences.

Escapists

If your child is a habitual daydreamer, is it because they have trouble with reality or because they're a genius? Both Einstein and Edison, if they were alive today, would likely be designated as having "learning difficulties," if not "special needs." But their tendency to drift off came together with a facility for fantasizing with a problem-solving purpose and they could apply their minds when they needed to.

Psychologist Eric Klinger identified a personality type he called "Heavy Daydreamers" and concluded that all the evidence refutes the belief that these types of people could be psychologically disturbed, or at least immature.

But obviously any tendency toward believing in a fantasy world at the expense of living in the real world does need looking at. If you are worried about your child's daydreaming proclivities, it's advisable to speak to teachers and/or a doctor. Hopefully you just have a highly imaginative child on your hands who could turn out to be a great thinker. Einstein said: "When I examine myself and my methods of thought, I come close to the conclusion that the gift of fantasy has meant more to me than my talent for absorbing positive knowledge."

3

SIT IN REVERIE AND WATCH THE
CHANGING COLORS OF THE
WAVES THAT BREAK UPON THE
IDLE SEASHORE OF THE MIND.

Henry Wadsworth Longfellow

How to make the most of it

Make some mind time

Yes, one of the wondrous things about daydreaming is that you can do it anytime, anywhere (and most of the time nobody else knows you're doing it!). But you can only daydream if your head isn't distracted by other stimuli.

Here are some ways to get some daydreaming time into your day.

Stymie the stimuli. Turn off that cellphone. Just sit on the bus and stare out of the window instead of ringing your best friend to talk about the fact that you're on the bus. Tell your boss you won't be available on the cellphone at all hours. Don't read a book or a newspaper. Be interested in where you go in your head. This might involve:

● Learning to say no and asking yourself why you're always so busy.

● Quietening your inner chatterbox, your critical voice—whatever it is that tells you that you shouldn't daydream, you're wasting time. Beating yourself up inside is not the same as daydreaming.

● Facing whatever comes up. Being busy can be a drug. When you're busy you don't have to think about your partner not talking to you, your mother looking ill, or how you're feeling about your job. But when you turn off the cellphone and put down the newspaper, those thoughts can come rushing in. As we already know from chapter one, you can daydream a solution.

ALL RELIGIONS WILL PASS, BUT THIS WILL REMAIN: SIMPLY SITTING IN A CHAIR AND LOOKING IN THE DISTANCE.

V. V. Rozanov

The art of doing nothing

Here are some ideas from creativity guru Julia Cameron on the power of stopping and doing nothing:

"Artists have stared out of windows and into their souls for a very long time. It is something in the staring out that enables us to do the looking-in. We forget that.

"So often we try to gird ourselves to face a harsh and difficult world when we might instead gentle both ourselves and our world just by slowing down. We worry rather than ruminate. We fret rather than speculate. Even football teams take time-outs, but it is so hard for us to do the same.

"We could take a cue from music here: 'rest' is a musical term for a pause between notes. Without that tiny pause, the torrent of notes can often be overwhelming. Without a rest in our lives, the torrent of our lives can be the same.

"Even God rested. Even waves rest. Even business titans close their doors and play with the secret toys on their desks. Our language of creativity knows this. We talk about 'the play of ideas,' but we still overwork and underplay and wonder why we feel so drained."

Cameron suggests setting yourself some homework of doing absolutely nothing for 15 minutes every day. Really doing nothing. Lie on the floor, put on some music that is "both calming and expansive," cross your arms over your chest, and let your train of thought take you where it will. Repeat this gentle phrase to yourself, over and over: "I am enough…I am enough…I am enough…."

This may not be daydreaming per se, but it may be what you need to do to calm down, slow down, and get into a daydreaming frame of mind.

Try it, you may like it.

An evening without an agenda

Why not try experimenting with an evening of doing absolutely zilch. Well, not absolutely—you can "do" those things that help you to daydream. Like a long, leisurely bath with candles. Or listening to music with a glass of fine wine.

But no video games. No playing Solitaire on your computer. No calling up your friends to gossip for hours. No TV and, no, not even any reading. What? It sounds like prison?

In her creativity course *The Artist's Way*, Cameron sets reading deprivation as an exercise for an entire week. If we're always filling our heads, according to her theory, we can have no idea what might come when we empty them. Apparently it's the exercise that meets with most resistance from her students…but also the one that produces the biggest breakthroughs. When you're not reading someone else's words, you can read yourself better.

Go for a walk

Rhythmic exercise, as we know, stimulates the right side of the brain. Walking is particularly conducive to daydreaming because being in wide open spaces somehow widens the mind. Even if you can only go for a walk in a city street, there's still the sky, which is as wide and open a space as space gets.

Also, when you are walking, things you see trigger daydreams, flights of fancy you might not have followed if just staring out of the window. There's something about this gentle looking out that creates magic within.

St. Augustine, himself a keen walker, said "solvitur ambulando"—"it is solved by walking." The "it" can be the answer to why your weakest team member is not pulling his or her weight, which comes as a flash of insight that hours fretting in front of the computer failed to achieve. Or the "it" can be the very thing to give your impossible-to-buy-for father for his birthday next week. Once you clear your mind by walking it's amazing what can pop in. And you can put a notebook in your pocket to jot down any strokes of genius that might suddenly come to you.

No power walking, mind. This kind of walking is a slower activity than rushing. When you walk—especially when you focus just on walking—your mind automatically slows down. Thoughts slow down. Daydreams appear. You feel better.

"Do" daydreaming

Daydreaming doesn't always have to mean doing nothing. Meditative activities encourage the mind to drift off even as the hands are busy doing something else. Making soup. Knitting, which is becoming fashionable again. Embroidery. Sketching. Walking. Swimming. These are meditative activities that allow you to daydream. Watching TV isn't one of them. Reading the newspaper isn't either. Choose something without input.

If you must have a task, make it a daydreaming task. If you just have to turn daydreaming into something to "do" this is how to do it.

I paint objects as I think them, not as I see them.

Pablo Picasso

The art of visualization

Don't fill up on other people's precooked daydreams. Create your own to be as beautiful as possible and see your life become a little lovelier as a result.

Visualization is "daydreaming with a purpose." Visualization is about using the power of the mind to help us get what we want by creating a clear visual picture of that thing, imbuing it with all the energy we can muster, and then letting life do the rest. "Energy follows thought" is a belief that is embraced by several spiritual traditions.

And if that all sounds a little airy-fairy, it's also true that world class athletes commonly use visualization as a crucial part of their winning strategies. They see themselves scoring that goal, winning that race, in their mind's eye. Tennis ace Arthur Ashe used the technique so much that it became second nature to him: "This is my way of relaxing. Other people call it lack of concentration, which is true. But I do it by habit, instinctively."

A daydream is a meal at which images are eaten. Some of us are gourmets, some gourmands, and a good many take their images precooked out of a can and swallow them down whole, absent-mindedly and with little relish.

W. H. Auden

I look out the window sometimes to seek the color of the shadows and the different greens in the trees, but when I get ready to paint I just close my eyes and imagine a scene.

Grandma Moses

Dream casting

Think of something you'd love to happen. Close your eyes and create a mental screen, like a movie screen, in your head just above your eyes. If you like you can visualize the whole movie theater, with yourself in the most comfortable seat, a box of popcorn in your lap. Now project up onto the screen the image of yourself enjoying that thing you'd love to happen. See it in Technicolor. Hear the words, the sounds, in surround sound. Smell the smells and feel the feelings. Imagine it in as much detail as you can. What are you wearing? What is the weather like?

When you've done this for a couple of minutes and you're sure that you've visualized everything as clearly as you possibly can, surround the whole picture with a pink bubble and let that bubble float off into the distance. Turn the movie screen into a pink bubble if you like, and watch it float off through the cinema's ceiling and off into the sky. In the imagination, anything is possible! Let it go. Don't obsess about it after this—just let it go, lightly and freely, floating far away.

All the visualization experts say that the trick with visualization is not just having the ability to see what you want clearly, but also having the ability to let it go and to not become overly attached to the outcome. Yes, you can bring the picture back into your mind from time to time, but in what visualization guru Shakti Gawain calls a "light gentle way." She says, "It's important not to feel like you're striving too hard for it or putting an excessive amount of energy into it—that would tend to hinder rather than help."

Know that you can come back to your own personal movie screen anytime you like. This technique can be used for anything from seeing yourself healthy to getting the job you dream of.

A place of your own

A powerful daydreaming technique is that of creating a personal sanctuary, a safe place that you can visit to do your daydreaming exercises. A place which can also become somewhere that will calm you every time you go there.

Close your eyes and envision a beautiful natural environment. It could be a real place you once went to—a beach or a field that you fell in love with. It can be a place in fiction or film—Frodo's garden in *Lord of the Rings*, a beach on the island in *Castaway*; or it can be somewhere you make up completely in your own daydreaming mind. You might want to make it feel totally secure by building a wall around it, or creating a force field that keeps other people away; or you could just see it as being huge and empty except for you.

Do anything you wish to make yourself feel at home there. You could include your pets, your children, or a favorite possession to be there with you. You could surround your sanctuary in protective light or have a waiter on hand to serve your favorite drink. Whatever you like—it's your fantasy!

From now on, this is your private sanctuary. You can close your eyes at any time and imagine yourself there and instantly feel calmer and more relaxed.

The mere cadence of the sentences, the subtle monotony of their music, so full as it was of complex refrains and movements elaborately repeated, produced in the mind of the lad, as he passed from chapter to chapter, a form of reverie, a malady of dreaming, that made him unconscious of the falling day and creeping shadows.

Oscar Wilde

Embody your vision

When you daydream, especially when envisioning something you want, it helps to anchor your vision in your body somehow. Daydreaming tends to take you out of your body, drifting off somewhere into hyperspace, but a creative visualization will be more effective if it's grounded in your body.

So try to keep part of your awareness on your solar plexus, your buttocks on the chair, or your feet on the floor as you drift off in your head. This really does change the quality of your daydreaming experience. Try it and see. Meanwhile, as you begin to bring your visualization into focus, notice how it makes your body feel. Do you relax? Do you feel a warm glow? Do you imagine yourself feeling good? The more vivid you can make the experience and the more it engages your bodily sensations, the more powerful its positive effect will be.

Meditation

Meditation is a kind of anti-daydreaming, if you like. In meditation you try to empty your brain of thoughts, rather than following them and seeing where they take you or consciously focusing them in a certain direction. You just notice your thoughts and let them pass. But, if you're interested in your daydreaming mind, meditation is a great tool.

The benefits of meditation are well researched. When you meditate, your heartbeat slows down, your metabolism slows down, your breathing slows down. Your whole system, in other words, relaxes. No wonder, then, that regular meditators look a good ten years younger on average than nonmeditators.

Meditation also brings your brain wave pattern into an alpha mode (see pages 12–13). Several studies have demonstrated that people who meditated for even as little as ten minutes a day showed increased alpha waves (the relaxed brain waves) and decreased anxiety and depression.

Meditation activates the sections of the brain in charge of the autonomic nervous system, which governs the functions in our bodies that we can't control, such as digestion and blood pressure, according to researchers at Harvard Medical School. These are also the functions that get messed around by stress. It makes sense, then, that easing these functions helps to ward off stress-related conditions, such as heart disease, digestive problems, and infertility.

Another study at the Maharishi School of Management in Fairfield, Iowa, found that people who had meditated for four months produced less of the stress hormone cortisol. They were better able to adapt to the pressures in their lives, wherever those pressures were coming from.

There are many different meditation techniques, from transcendental to zen and all those in between. But, basically, you are meditating if you sit quietly, with your eyes closed and just focus on your breath going in and going out. Thoughts may intrude, but you don't become attached to the thought, you just return your focus to your breathing.

You are also meditating if you are walking—eyes open, obviously!—and just focusing on your feet hitting the ground one at a time.

Zen Buddhists call the meditative attitude "mindfulness"— your mind is full only of the activity you are engaged in. If you are stirring a pot of soup, you are mindful of the action of stirring the soup. If you are sitting quietly, eyes closed, focused on your breath or a one-word mantra ("calm" is a good one), then you are mindful only of sitting, breathing, and repeating the word.

I WAS TRYING TO DAYDREAM, BUT MY MIND KEPT WANDERING.

Steven Wright

The awareness continuum

This exercise, from Gestalt Therapy (the word Gestalt means complete or whole), is similar to meditating. And like meditating it's a kind of anti-daydreaming, but it isn't logical, linear thinking either.

All you do—and you can do this out loud or in your head—is focus on what you see, feel, think, sense, and only that. So, for example, you might say, "I'm looking at the sky and it's very blue today with hardly a cloud and I'm hearing that woman shouting at her dog and I'm looking at the dog and I'm feeling sad because I'm remembering my dog who died when I was 14, and I'm sensing how my toes feel nice and warm in my new woollen socks and I'm feeling my feet on the ground as I'm walking…."

And so on.

The trick is not to identify with any thoughts or feelings that come into your head, but simply notice what is there.

Practitioners who work with this technique say it's brilliant for treating anxiety and obsession, given that it stops you obsessing about the past and worrying about the future and it anchors you solidly in the now.

Daydream your decisions

This is a powerful technique for decision making that bypasses the logical mind, which tells you what you should do, and gets at what you really want to do. Feelings often hold our true desires.

Sit in a quiet place and close your eyes. One at a time, imagine each scenario connected with each decision. Let's say you have to decide whether to accept a job offer, or stay where you are. Choose one scenario and literally daydream yourself into that new job. Remember to use all your senses to make it as vivid as possible. Notice how things look, how you feel, what you see, hear, touch, and smell. When you've done this for a few minutes, let it go and conjure up a vision of staying in your job,

having turned the other job down. Again make it as vivid as possible, do it for a few minutes until you feel yourself in the scene, and let it go.

Now open your eyes and think about how the two scenarios went. Often you can make an instant decision, based on how you felt. I used this technique once to choose whether or not to take a new job, and I was powerfully struck by how excited I felt in the scenario where I'd taken the job, even though I felt a little scared, too; and by how jealous I felt in the second scenario of the person who would be doing the job if I had turned it down. I took the job. And it was absolutely the right decision.

Coleridge and "Kubla Khan"

The poet Samuel Taylor Coleridge said one of his most famous works was "composed in a sort of Reverie." He was famously something of an opium addict, and this reverie was drug-induced (though Coleridge said he'd taken "an anodyne" in consequence of a "slight indisposition"). But nonetheless, the poem, written in 1798 and inspired by a book on Egypt, called *Purchas's Pilgrimage*, is a thing of great beauty.

> **In Xanadu did Kubla Khan**
> **A stately pleasure-dome decree:**
> **Where Alph, the sacred river, ran**
> **Through caverns measureless to man**
> **Down to a sunless sea.**

This opening is generally considered to be one of the most beautiful in English literature and it promises great things as the poem proceeds. It paints a picture of the mighty ruler Kubla Khan and his Elysian paradise, with a famous depiction of a poet—"His flashing eyes, his floating hair"—that became one of the defining images of the Romantic movement. Coleridge said he dreamed some two to three hundred lines in his poem-as-dream and was eagerly writing them down when he returned to full consciousness.

The finished work is, in fact, a mere 18 lines long. The writer describes one of the worst-timed interruptions ever:

At this moment he was unfortunately called out by a person on business from Porlock, and detained by him above an hour, and on his return to his room, found, to his no small surprise and mortification, that though he retained some vague and dim recollection of the general purport of his vision, yet, with the exception of some eight or ten scattered lines and images, all the rest had passed away like the images of the surface of a stream into which a stone has been cast.

Sadly, the rest of his opium-induced stroke of daydreaming genius is lost to literature.

I LIKE NONSENSE, IT WAKES UP THE BRAIN CELLS.
FANTASY IS A NECESSARY INGREDIENT IN LIVING,
IT'S A WAY OF LOOKING AT LIFE THROUGH
THE WRONG END OF A TELESCOPE. WHICH IS
WHAT I DO, AND THAT ENABLES YOU TO LAUGH
AT LIFE'S REALITIES.

Dr. Theodore Geisel, a.k.a. Dr. Seuss

Daydream your deepest desires

If you're not the Billy Liar type and you're not in the habit of daydreaming yourself as some other more glamorous, courageous, heroic person, this exercise can be a revelation. Take a piece of paper and write down the sentence: "Secretly, I would love to…." Then allow yourself to daydream.

The ending might be something like:
- go bungee jumping
- tell my boss I've been headhunted
- do an art course
- take a year off to go traveling
- live by the sea
- join a dating agency

Do this 10 times. The answers can be as naughty, silly, outrageous, or just plain impossible as you like. It's a secret list, remember? Now pick just a couple of your answers and daydream them. Make a mental movie of you actually fulfilling this dream and make that movie as vivid as possible. Later, if you like, you can think about these dreams and, indeed, all the dreams on your list. Useful questions to ask yourself are:

- What is it about this dream that excites me?
- Why can't I don't do this?
- What information does this offer about myself and my life?
- What kind of fear stops me from doing this?
- Is there any small step I could take to incorporate the quality of this dream into my life?

So if, for example, it's bungee jumping, does this indicate that your life is lacking a sense of thrill? How could you add more excitement to your life, whether you bungee jump or not?

Got a problem?

Haven't we all. This is a technique for blasting you out of your usual problem-solving strategies and opening up possibilities that might never have occurred to you otherwise. I've used this technique in the training I do with journalists and it works well with people management problems—what can I do about this reporter's negative attitude? It also helps when we're thinking of ideas for articles or how to implement a relaunch. It's particularly fun to do with a friend or your partner—and laughing about your problems always makes you feel better about them too.

Get a huge sheet of paper and write "sublime" in the top-left corner and "ridiculous" in the top-right corner. Now draw a large V shape on the paper with the top two tips of the V hitting each word, so the base point comes between the words in the middle at the bottom. Now daydream solutions to the problem that would fit the description "sublime" and write them in the space under the word. The most sublime solution should go right in the top-left corner, not-quite-so-sublime ones should go underneath, veering toward the point in the middle, which represents solutions neither particularly sublime nor especially ridiculous. Now daydream a few "ridiculous" solutions and do the same with them. Truly ridiculous ones go in the top-right corner, any little-bit ridiculous ideas go farther down toward the middle and, as before, in the middle go those solutions that are more realistic.

Here's an example. Let's say you're feeling cramped where you live and need more space. A "sublime" solution might be to move to a bigger house or flat, but you can't afford that. Nonetheless, you write it under "sublime"—what we're doing is looking at all the possibilities as a prelude to choosing one, but it's always useful to know what your best possible outcome would be. A "ridiculous" solution might be to move the kitchen into the garden shed. Write that in the top-right corner. OK, it's mad and not workable—it's a ridiculous solution. But even the most ridiculous ideas can have a grain of inspiration in them. OK, you won't use the shed to put the kitchen in, but is there some other way you can make better use of the shed? Build a bigger shed? And so on.

As you fill in all the possible solutions you can daydream, you will land on one that is just perfect. It's a marvelous cure for those times when you get stuck in black-and-white thinking: the only thing we can do is move and we can't do that, so… and so on, round and round in circles. Go in a V-shape instead!

THROW YOUR DREAMS INTO SPACE LIKE A KITE, AND YOU DO NOT KNOW WHAT IT WILL BRING BACK, A NEW LIFE, A NEW FRIEND, A NEW LOVE, A NEW COUNTRY.

Anaïs Nin

What do you wish for?

This is another good exercise for anchoring your daydreams and seeing if it's feasible to try to make any of them come true. Some of the answers may be similar to those on page 76, like "I wish I had the courage to go bungee jumping," but most will be completely different.

Take a piece of paper, write "wish list" at the top, and number down the left side from 1–50. Now just let go and write down all your wishes. Yes, 50 of them. You'll find they really flow at first, but then there may be some sticky patches where you can't think of anything—try thinking about if money wasn't an issue—would you go back to college and study English Literature? History of Art? Psychology? Would you buy a boat and sail single-handedly around the world? Would you just take six months off, go on a long holiday, and do absolutely nothing? Would you write a novel? Set up a ballet school? Breed Dobermans? Daydream laterally!

What do these daydreams tell you about where you're at right now? Are they all about getting some time to yourself? Wanting more from your relationships? Quitting your job? Escape? Making more of a contribution to the world? Improving your relationships with your family?

Scan the list and see which ones have the biggest feelings attached to them. Do any make you feel sad because they've been wishes for so long that you despair of them ever coming true? Most importantly, is there a theme?

Now you can think seriously and honestly about how much you want to make any of them happen, and whether you are ready to do what it takes. Sometimes we believe we want something, but when we make ourselves think through all it would demand, and its consequences, we realize we would rather settle for life as it is, imperfect though it may be.

Daydream you're old

Usually when we daydream we see ourselves as young, famous, successful, rich. Or just as we are now but coping with life in a superhuman way. But what about daydreaming the end of your life?

Imagine you're eighty. Has your life turned out the way you thought it would? What advice would you give yourself now? What do you regret—if anything? What do you wish you hadn't been so afraid of? What way in which you limit yourself now do you wish you had freed yourself?

Daydreaming the future can unravel mysteries about the present. It reveals priorities, time-wasters, and energy-drains.

More questions to reflect on:
- If you were to die tomorrow what's the one thing you'd like your legacy to be?
- If you were to die tomorrow, what's the one thing you think people would say about you? Say you'd achieved? Say was the main quality you had?

One quality of daydreaming is to take you out of your everyday life. Daydreams like these, following avenues like these, can take you to some very interesting places and lead to some fascinating conclusions. All psychologists say awareness is the first step to changing anything, if we wish to make a change.

Keep an ideas journal

Once you start noticing your daydreams, your creativity may go off the scale. So to make sure you don't lose any precious insights, ideas, or inspirations, write down any ideas that come to you. This doesn't mean you have to act on them, but by recording them all in a journal you may be able to use them in the years to come or they may spark another round of useful daydreaming in you.

Buy yourself a really special little notebook just for this incredibly private information.

I am a dreamer of words, of written words. I think I am reading; a word stops me. I leave the page. The syllables of the word begin to move around. Stressed accents begin to invert. The word abandons its meaning like an overload which is too heavy and prevents dreaming. Then words take on other meanings as if they had the right to be young. And the words wander away, looking in the nooks and crannies of vocabulary for new company, bad company.

Gaston Bachelard

Think about submodalities

This is a technique from Neuro Linguistic Programming, a branch of psychology that emphasizes the importance of having a clear outcome in your head in order to make anything happen. NLP holds that there are three types of people: those who primarily relate to the world through their eyes (visual type), those who do so through their ears (auditory type), and those who do so through their senses and feelings (kinesthetic type). Think about what happens when you daydream. Do you mostly see pictures, hear conversations in your head, or "feel" the things you're daydreaming about? Most people have two of these functions quite strongly, with the third weaker.

If you have a daydream you want to make real, a goal you want to visualize, NLP practitioners would advise playing with the details of the picture—what they call the "submodalities" and making them brighter.

So, if you can see a picture in your mind's eye, how well developed is it? Is it black and white? Technicolor? In sharp focus or fuzzy? Could you make the images brighter or more pastel? Is the result better or worse? Does it run like a movie or is it static? Do the images move quickly or slowly? If you speed them up or slow them down, is the result better or worse? Whose eyes are you seeing the picture with—yours or an onlookers? How does changing that change the picture?

If you're an auditory type and can "hear" your daydream, is it loud or quiet? Calm or dramatic? Pitched high or low? With background music or without? What happens if you change these details?

If you can "feel" your daydream, is the sensation internal or external? Gentle or intense? Intermittent or continuous? Speedy or slow? Again, what happens if you change these things—does it get better or worse?

It can be fun to play with these "submodalities." One NLP practitioner, who made sure she created a clear picture of herself crossing the finishing line when she was training for the London Marathon, says: "The image, which I made very bright with a blue sky, kept me going not just during the marathon itself, but on those dull, gray mornings when I was training and the world looked nothing like my image."

Make yesterday perfect

Remember the film *Groundhog Day*? When Bill Murray lives the same day over and over again until he finally gets it right? This exercise is similar—an antidote to those times when life feels out of control. Basically, you take yesterday and think it through, remembering all the things that happened and how they happened. You can write it out—always therapeutic—or just remember. Now think through or write out yesterday again, but this time right all the wrongs. Imagine yourself arriving at that meeting on time, rather than ten minutes late. Which maybe involves imagining the train flowing smoothly along the track rather than getting stuck in the tunnel....

This exercise helps you feel more in control of your life, helps you generate choices about the small rituals and routines of life, and can help you live more effectively.

Make tomorrow perfect

Mental rehearsal really does work. If you imagine yourself running, even while you're couch-potatoing on the sofa, a polygraph machine would be able to pick up electrical activity in your leg muscles, as Pennsylvanian sports psychologists Dorothy Harris and William Robinson have shown. They found these signals would be strongest if you imagine moving your muscles in ways you have already practiced in reality. Similarly, basketball stars can improve their scores by imagining getting balls in hoops when they're not actually playing.

So, if you're planning to get fit, you can literally start yourself off from the sofa. But as with physical rehearsal, so with mental rehearsal, too. Behavioral psychologists have long used a technique called "covert rehearsal" to improve their clients' coping skills—their ability to assert themselves, for example. So if you have a trying meeting with your boss coming up, spend a few minutes imagining that meeting going well. See yourself as clear, witty, and direct, and feeling good, and see your boss with a great big grin on his face. This positive outcome will be much more likely to come true than if you imagine the worst. And it really does work—as with anything, practice makes perfect, even when the practice is only imaginary.

Write out your daydreams

If you're keen on writing, write out a daydream. It doesn't have to be a story with a beginning, middle, and end, though it might turn out that way. And it doesn't have to be a beautiful, well-written piece of writing. Just try putting pen to paper without a specific goal apart from the very gentle one of jotting down some daydreams. I say pen to paper rather than fingers to keyboard because writing by hand kicks the right side of the brain into action more effectively than typing. But if you can daydream and type at the same time, that's fine too.

If you wish, you can take these sentence prompts to help you:
- I imagine…
- If I were lost on a desert island…
- Once upon a time…
- The place I'd most like to travel to is…
- In my alternative life I …

It can be a very powerful tool to write down your daydreams—actually to see them in black and white on the page. These are my dreams! This is where I go when I daydream and I simply have my own mind to myself. Keep them and, years, or even just months from now, you may read them back and be amazed at yourself. You'll certainly be entertained.

One thing you've never dreamed of

OK, you've done a fair amount of daydreaming by now, even if you haven't done any of the exercises. Here's a question from the coaching world that may get that gray matter well and truly exercised. When you are daydreaming about how your life might be, is there one thing you have never dared to consider, but that you'd like to? What would matter so much to you that you'd give up whatever you're struggling over right now to get it? The answer might just be life-changing.

Essential oils for daydreaming

In 1985 research into the mind-altering qualities of essential oils was done in Japan by Dr. Shizuo Torii, who found, by measuring brain waves, that some aromas have a stimulating effect and some a relaxing effect.

Aromatherapy, as a form of herbalism, has been practiced since ancient times. Our modern form dates from 1928 when French chemist René-Maurice Gattefosse burned his arm and instinctively plunged it into a nearby vat of lavender essential oil. The pain lessened immediately and the arm healed surprisingly quickly, triggering a whole new area of alternative therapy.

Essential oils can be absorbed through the skin, or via inhalation, and carried throughout the body by the lymph and circulatory system.

The guidelines for using them are:

● The only oil that can be used neat on the skin is lavender—and then only a little. All the others must be diluted in a base oil, such as almond, jojoba, or grapeseed, or added to the bath, diluted first in a little milk.

● Use only oils you like the smell of. If you hate an oil, it's not going to work for you—remember that this should be a good experience. Choose the oils that give you pleasure.

● Certain oils should be avoided during pregnancy. These are angelica, basil, cedarwood, chamomile (during the first trimester), clary sage, fennel, frankincense (first trimester), galbanum, jasmine, juniper, marjoram, myrrh, nutmeg, peppermint (first trimester), rosemary, tagetes, and thyme. Some aromatherapists advise against using oils on the skin at all during pregnancy and only advocate using them via an essential oil burner. This is an easier option if you're at all concerned.

● Don't use basil or peppermint in the bath.

Daydreaming with a purpose:

Daydreaming and confusion are not one and the same thing. If you're wanting to improve your concentration so you can daydream or do a creative visualization on a particular issue, here are the essential oils that can help:

cardamom, ginger, black pepper, bergamot, geranium, petitgrain, grapefruit, basil, rosemary, peppermint, cypress, juniper, pine, thyme, lavender.

Daydreaming without a purpose:

If you just want to relax, let go, and allow your mind to wander where it will, here are the oils for you:

bergamot, lavender, mandarin, chamomile, sandalwood, vetiver, neroli, rose otto, cedarwood, geranium, melissa, juniper, frankincense, clary sage, patchouli.

Enjoy being bored

If you create more time for daydreaming, for "doing nothing" in your life, it might feel uncomfortable at first. You may even experience physical and emotional symptoms of withdrawal as you slow down and give yourself some quiet time to yourself. You may sleep more, or less. You may be a buzz with energy. You may even become a little depressed—momentarily—as you realize just how mad your life has become.

You may—quite possibly—get bored.

Don't get too down though—the body, mind, and spirit must go through a few changes when adjusting from a life of "busy-ness" and mental clutter to a life with space to breathe. A space that may feel weird at first but offers huge payoffs in terms of relaxation and mental ease.

If you're bored, stay with being bored for a little while before you rush back to the cellphone and the TV. Boredom can be what happens just before you feel peace. Or it can be a signal that a few of your daydreams need to come true.

Sometimes, in a summer morning, having taken my accustomed bath, I sat in my sunny doorway from sunrise till noon, rapt in reverie.

Henry David Thoreau

The Buddha

Siddhartha Gautama, a Nepalese prince who gave up his life of privilege to go off and become a monk, attained Enlightenment sitting under the Bodhi tree. He vowed never to leave the position until he found Truth. He claimed he had realized complete Awakening and insight into the nature and cause of human suffering along with the steps necessary to eliminate it.

OK, he was meditating, not daydreaming. But neither was he running around doing the supermarket shopping while simultaneously organizing his stocks and shares via his cellphone. Or whatever the fifth century equivalent would be. And you're not telling me that he didn't have the odd fantasy under that tree.

Turning a daydream into reality

We've talked a lot about daydreaming, how it's good, necessary, enlightening, and relaxing. But what if your daydreaming exercises have uncovered a fantasy you'd like to act on or a dream you want to turn into reality?

Well, you can now use many of the techniques in this book to speed this process along.

If it's not obvious to you right now, you could try using the exercises on pages 61, 64, 71, 76, 78, 80, 81, 83 and 88 in this chapter to get clear about what you want.

Choose a daydream that really tugs at your heartstrings and you fervently want to make happen.

Use the visualization technique to create a clear picture of how it's going to be once you've made this dream come true. Put your visualization in the present tense: this is how I am feeling and thinking, now this dream is coming true.

Ask yourself: what small step could I take to make this happen? You could always use the "sublime and ridiculous" exercise (page 78) to get clear about all the steps you could take. Just do it! Take that first small step.

One of the biggest blocks to making our dreams a reality—even when we believe we truly deserve the thing we want and truly could do it or have it if only we had the time/money/whatever—is the idea that it has to happen all at once. You have to go from how you are now to being a great artist by tomorrow. But anyone who has ever reached any goal will tell you it was achieved in small increments, one small step at a time. You research the art courses. You buy some pencils. You join the art class. You rent the studio. And so on, and so on…all the way to the Museum of Modern Art.

Happy dreaming!

Picture credits

Cover © Bill Miles/CORBIS; Page 2 © Charles Gupton/CORBIS; Pages 8–9 © as cover; Page 11 © Russell Underwood/CORBIS; Pages 16–17 © royalty free/CORBIS; Pages 22–23 © John Henley/CORBIS; Pages 30–31 © Tibor Bognár/CORBIS; Page 35 © Allana Wesley White/CORBIS; Pages 36–37 © Eleonora Ghioldi/CORBIS; Page 43 © Lou Chardonnay/CORBIS; Page 48 © Rob Lewine/CORBIS; Page 53 © Barbara Peacock/CORBIS; Pages 54–55 © Ariel Skelley/CORBIS; Page 62 © C/B Productions/CORBIS; Pages 74–75 © LWA-JDC/CORBIS; Page 82 © LWA-Stephen Welstead/CORBIS; Page 95 © Bob Krist/CORBIS